Monitoring Kittlitz's and Marbled Murrelets in Glacier Bay National Park and Preserve

2009 Annual Report

Natural Resource Technical Report NPS/SEAN/NRTR—2011/440

Steven T. Hoekman

Institute of Arctic Biology
University of Alaska
Fairbanks, AK, 99775

Brendan J. Moynahan

Southeast Alaska Network, Inventory and Monitoring Program
National Park Service
3100 National Park Road
Juneau, AK, 99801

Mark S. Lindberg

Institute of Arctic Biology
University of Alaska
Fairbanks, AK, 99775

March 2011

U.S. Department of the Interior
National Park Service
Natural Resource Program Center
Fort Collins, Colorado

The National Park Service, Natural Resource Program Center publishes a range of reports that address natural resource topics of interest and applicability to a broad audience in the National Park Service and others in natural resource management, including scientists, conservation and environmental constituencies, and the public.

The Natural Resource Technical Report Series is used to disseminate results of scientific studies in the physical, biological, and social sciences for both the advancement of science and the achievement of the National Park Service mission. The series provides contributors with a forum for displaying comprehensive data that are often deleted from journals because of page limitations.

All manuscripts in the series receive the appropriate level of peer review to ensure that the information is scientifically credible, technically accurate, appropriately written for the intended audience, and designed and published in a professional manner.

This report received formal peer review by subject-matter experts who were not directly involved in the collection, analysis, or reporting of the data, and whose background and expertise put them on par technically and scientifically with the authors of the information.

Views, statements, findings, conclusions, recommendations, and data in this report do not necessarily reflect views and policies of the National Park Service, U.S. Department of the Interior. Mention of trade names or commercial products does not constitute endorsement or recommendation for use by the U.S. Government.

This report is available from the Southeast Alaska Network (http://science.nature.nps.gov/im/units/sean/Default.aspx) and the Natural Resource Publications Management website (http://www.nature.nps.gov/publications/NRPM).

Please cite this publication as:

Hoekman, S. T., B. J. Moynahan, and M. S. Lindberg. 2011. Monitoring Kittlitz's and marbled murrelets in Glacier Bay National Park: 2009 annual report. Natural Resource Technical Report NPS/SEAN/NRTR—2011/440. National Park Service, Fort Collins, Colorado.

NPS 132/107034, March 2011

Contents

Figures

Tables

vi

Executive Summary

The Kittlitz's murrelet (*Brachyramphus brevirostris*) is a rare seabird endemic to Alaska and northeastern Russia that is closely associated with glacially-influenced habitats and breeds in several national parks, including Glacier Bay, Kenai Fjords, and Wrangell-St. Elias. Recent evidence suggesting declines in global and Alaska populations prompted listing of this species as a candidate (Priority 2) for protection under the Endangered Species Act. However, differences in survey and analytic methods have contributed to considerable uncertainty about population status and trend.

The Southeast Alaska Network (SEAN) seeks to develop and implement long-term monitoring of Kittlitz's murrelets in Glacier Bay National Park and Preserve, because Glacier Bay proper (hereafter "Glacier Bay") hosts a substantial proportion of the global breeding population. Prior research in Glacier Bay using strip transect methods has suggested a declining population, but uncertainty remains because of several challenges to effective monitoring: large spatial and temporal variation in populations, incomplete detection of these elusive birds, difficulty distinguishing the morphologically similar marbled murrelet (*B. marmoratus*), and complications in sampling convoluted fjord topography. SEAN has embarked on a two-year effort of evaluating alternative sampling and analytic strategies for monitoring. In 2009, we focused on testing current survey methods and better tailoring field and analytic methods to suit our study system. Specifically, our objectives were to 1) implement boat-based line transect surveys to estimate abundance and distribution of Kittlitz's murrelets, and secondarily of marbled murrelets, in Glacier Bay, 2) test the critical assumption of complete detection near the transect center line ("center line"), 3) compare line versus strip transect methods, 4) assess performance of 1 versus 2 observers, and 5) extend analytic methods to account for incomplete detection and species identification.

During July 2009, we implemented a stratified, random, spatially-balanced sampling design with reasonable coverage of Glacier Bay and sampled 219 km on 53 transects. We estimated detection probability near the center line as 0.94 (SE = 0.03). Relative to 1 observer, 2 observers had 56% higher encounter rates, had >20% higher probability of species identification, and better met assumptions of line transect sampling. We identified 47% of observed murrelets to species and estimated detection of murrelet groups at 150 m from the center line was <50%. Using line transect methods in concert with novel analytic methods accounting for incomplete detection and identification, we estimated an abundance of 13,124 ± 4,602 ($\bar{x}$ ± SE) Kittlitz's and 28,978 ± 4,077 marbled murrelets on the water in our 1,092 km^2 study area in July 2009. Corresponding estimates using strip transect methods were smaller >50% and were ~10% less precise because of bias and error associated with incomplete detection and species identification. Distribution of Kittlitz's murrelet was patchy. Estimated densities were almost twice as high in high relative to low density strata, which increased precision of abundance estimates. But, a transect with very high density in the low density strata decreased effectiveness of stratification.

Based on our 2009 results, we identify a number of recommendations, all of which will be incorporated into the revised project design for 2010. We recommend continued use of line transect methods, analytic methods accounting for incomplete species identification, use of 2 versus 1 survey observers, spatially-balanced sampling, and allocation of sampling effort proportional to expected densities of Kittlitz's murrelets. Our primary suggested improvements are analytic methods not requiring *a priori* stratification relative to density and decreasing variability in transect length. We also emphasize benefits of observer training to increase skill in species identification and distance estimation. We found no unbiased methods for sampling flying birds.

Acknowledgments

We are indebted to our boat captain J. Smith. W. F. Johnson and L. S. Sharman provided indispensable assistance with field operations and data management. We thank S. M. Gende and G. V. Hilderbrand for comments on versions of this report and M. J. Conroy, J. L. Laake, and P. M. Lukacs for comments on our methods. H. Coletti, B. Eichenlaub, S. M. Gende, J. I. Hodges, M. D. Kirchhoff, M. L. Kissling, C. Smith, and W. L. Thompson contributed advice and/or logistic support.

Introduction

The Vital Signs program being implemented by the Southeast Alaska Network (SEAN) of the National Park Service seeks to monitor status and trends of ecosystem components or processes selected for their ecological and management significance (Moynahan et al. 2008). Reflecting a setting in the northern Alexander Archipelago, SEAN monitoring focuses on marine ecosystems.

The Kittlitz's murrelet is a rare seabird endemic to Alaska and northeastern Russia (Day et al. 1999) that is closely associated with glacially-influenced habitats (Kuletz et al. 2003), often foraging near outflows of tidewater glaciers (Day and Nigro 2000) and nesting in recently deglaciated areas with sparse vegetation (Day 1995). A significant population breeds in Glacier Bay National Park and Preserve, with lesser populations in other national parks including Kenai Fjords and Wrangell-St. Elias. Selection of this species for long-term monitoring as one of twelve priority Vital Signs arose from concern about population declines and belief that populations directly relate to drivers of ecosystem change that SEAN has also committed to monitoring (i.e., glacial dynamics, climate change, human activity). Recent evidence suggesting declines of global and Glacier Bay populations prompted listing of Kittlitz's murrelets as a candidate (Priority 2) for protection under the Endangered Species Act (USFWS 2010). However, large uncertainty in population status and trend remains, in part because of differences in survey and analytic methods among prior studies (USFWS 2010, Hoekman et al. 2011b).

Development of a monitoring protocol is informed by substantial prior research in Glacier Bay on seabirds in general, and Kittlitz's and more numerous marbled murrelets in particular (Agler et al. 1998, Lindell 2005, Romano et al. 2007, Drew et al. 2008, Kirchhoff 2008). Kittlitz's murrelets typically have been highly aggregated within Glacier Bay, but distributions of both species have varied dramatically both within and among breeding seasons. Indices to abundance have suggested a decline in the population of Kittlitz's murrelets, but substantial uncertainty remains because of differences in sampling designs, survey methods, and analytic methods among studies. Additional to the need for standardized methods, successful monitoring must adequately address challenges inherent to the study system. Large variation in abundance and distributions of murrelets decreases precision of abundance estimates, and hence the level of sampling effort required for effective monitoring may be unsustainable (Agler et al. 1998, Kissling et al. 2007, Drew et al. 2008). The convoluted topography of Glacier Bay's fjords complicates both representative sampling of the study area and defining transects with suitable shape, length, and orientation. Murrelets can be difficult to detect, because they are small, cryptic, and often fly or dive when approached by vessels (Agness et al. 1998, Mack et al. 2002, Lukacs et al. 2010). In addition, observers cannot always reliably distinguish the morphologically similar Kittlitz's and marbled murrelets, and proportion of unidentified murrelets during surveys has ranged from 0-50%. Strip transect methods (Williams et al. 2002) typically used for surveys in Glacier Bay have not adequately accounted for detection probability, incomplete species identification, or flying birds; this has resulted in introduction of large and variable bias to abundance estimates (Hoekman et al. 2011a,b). Line transect methods (Buckland et al. 2001) allow estimation of detection probability, but assumptions of this method have rarely been assessed for birds (Bachler and Liechti 2007).

To address these concerns, SEAN has embarked on a two-year effort of evaluating alternative sampling and analytic strategies for monitoring. In 2009, we conducted a pilot study focusing on testing current survey methods and better tailoring field and analytic methods to suit our study system. In 2010, we introduced refinements suggested by 2009 results (Hoekman et al. 2011a).

Our monitoring design and survey methods were driven by our predominant interest in Kittlitz's murrelets. However, because of the importance of distinguishing between coexisting Kittlitz's and marbled murrelets, we present results on the abundance and distribution for both species.

Our objectives for the 2009 pilot surveys were to implement boat-based line transect surveys to estimate abundance of Kittlitz's murrelets (and secondarily of marbled murrelets) using a sampling design that provided reasonable coverage of Glacier Bay and that ameliorated effects of spatial variation in murrelet distributions. We used field experiments to test the critical assumption of line transect methods of complete detection near the center line, to assess performance of 1 vs. 2 observers, and to try alternative methods for surveying flying murrelets. We also extended analytic methods for line transect methods to better account for incomplete detection and identification of murrelets to species, and we assessed performance of line versus strip transects.

Methods

Study area and species

Rapid glacial retreat over the last 250 years has exposed Glacier Bay, a narrow, ~100 km long fjord in Southeast Alaska, USA (Fig. 1). The upper reaches receive discharge of turbid fresh water and ice from numerous glaciers. Repeated glacial advance and retreat have created complex bathymetry, including numerous deep basins and sills, resulting in large variation in depth, tidal influence, water temperature, salinity, turbidity, and productivity (Robards et al. 2003). Our study are encompassed 1,092 km^2 of Glacier Bay proper (consisting of waters north of the mouth of Icy Strait) and excluded areas too small to allow safe and easy passage, non-motorized areas, and critical habitat areas (Fig. 2).

Kittlitz's and marbled murrelets are morphologically and behaviorally similar and cannot always be distinguished in the field (Fig. 3). When approached within 50-100 m, murrelets typically attempt to evade detection by swimming, flying, or diving (Agness et al. 2008, Lukacs et al. 2010). Evasive and foraging dives often persist for 20-30 s or more.

Sampling design

Large spatial variation observed for murrelets in Glacier Bay and elsewhere (Kissling et al. 2007, Drew et al. 2008, Kirchhoff 2008) can impede effective monitoring because this variation often is paramount to estimated precision of abundance estimates (Fewster et al. 2009). Use of a Generalized Random Tessellation Stratified (GRTS) sampling design allowed us to diminish deleterious effects of spatial variation by providing a random yet spatially-balanced sample. Additionally, we delineated 3 areas where past densities were ~4x higher than elsewhere in the study area; these high density strata received twice the sampling intensity of low density strata (Fig 3). We preferred linear transects, which facilitate precise replication of surveys (Kirchhoff *In Review*). To avoid placing transects parallel to the observed density gradient of murrelets relative to water depth (Drew et al. 2008, Kirchhoff 2008, Kirchhoff *In Review*), we oriented transects perpendicular to the local prevailing shoreline (Fig. 2). Most transects ran shore-to-shore, but some traversing the widest portion of Glacier Bay had endpoints at mid-bay to maintain recommended transect lengths of <8 km (Drew et al. 2008).

Field methods

We used distance sampling methods (Buckland et al. 2001) to conduct boat-based line transect surveys during 8-15 July 2009 aboard the R/V Capelin and R/V Boomer. We surveyed between 8:00 and 17:00 with 1-3 observer(s) in the bow using 10x binoculars and 1 crew member as a dedicated data recorder. Viewing height was ~2.5 m above the water. Maximum survey speed was 10 km/h, and we reduced speed when encountering numerous murrelets. When confidence in identification was high, we classified murrelets to species. Otherwise, we classified murrelets as unidentified. We only recorded observations of groups (defined as murrelets of one species class separated by <3 m between individuals) initially located on the water. We did not sample when Beaufort sea state exceeded 3 or when visibility was <100 m. Prior to and during surveys, we trained observers in distance estimation using laser range finders to determine distances to small buoys and seabirds. We conducted 2 field experiments when sufficient personnel allowed. We assessed performance relative to number of observers by randomly assigning 1 or 2 primary

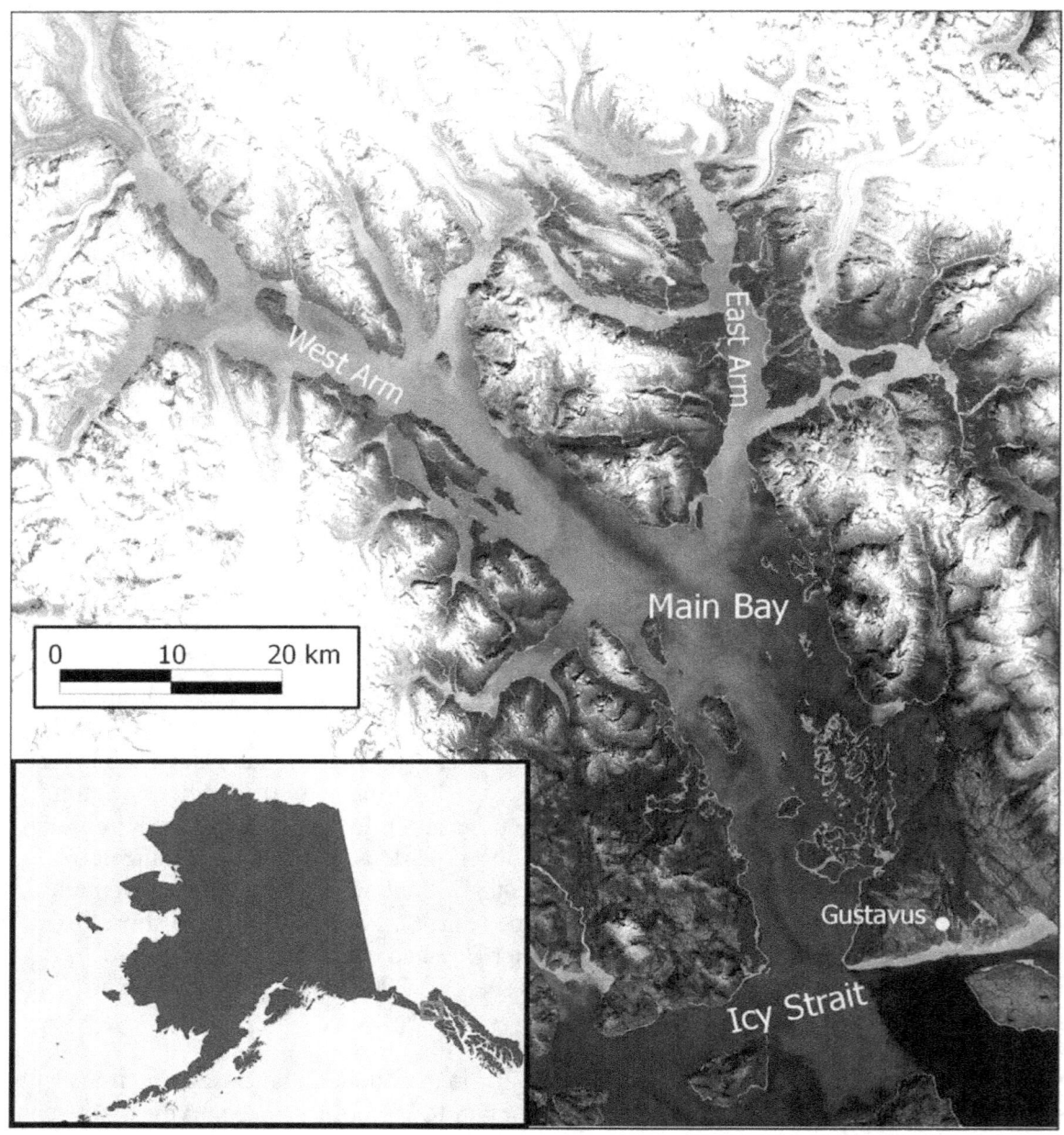

Figure 1. Glacier Bay proper encompasses waters north of Icy Strait and is composed of a broad main bay and numerous narrows fjords.

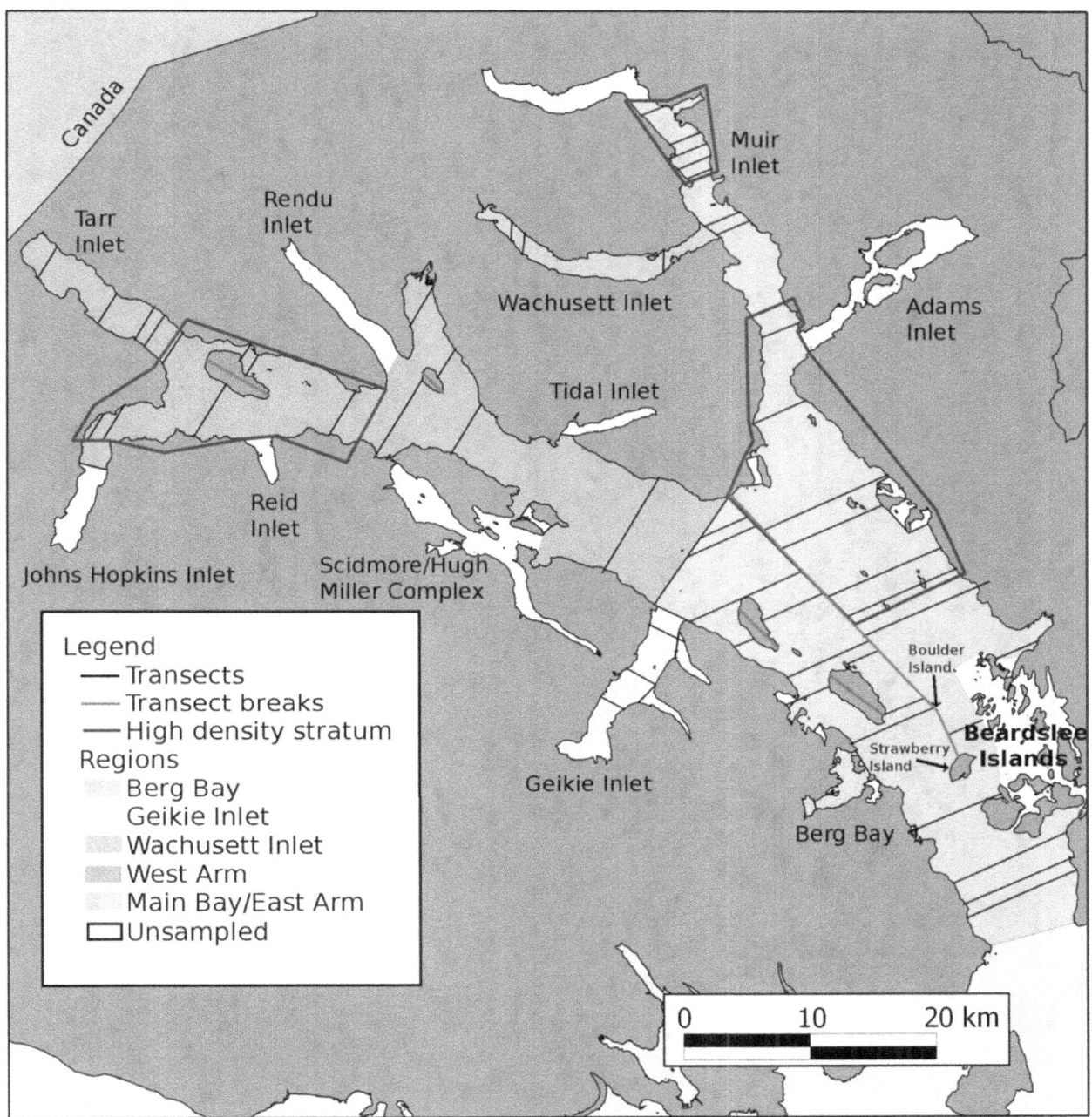

Figure 2. Sampling scheme for surveys of murrelets within Glacier Bay during July 2009. Regions were defined solely for the purposes of this study based upon prevailing shoreline orientation. Line transects were oriented perpendicular to the prevailing shoreline in each region. Transects extended from shore to shore, except where split by breaks. The 3 areas comprising the high density stratum had twice the sampling probability relative to elsewhere in the study area.

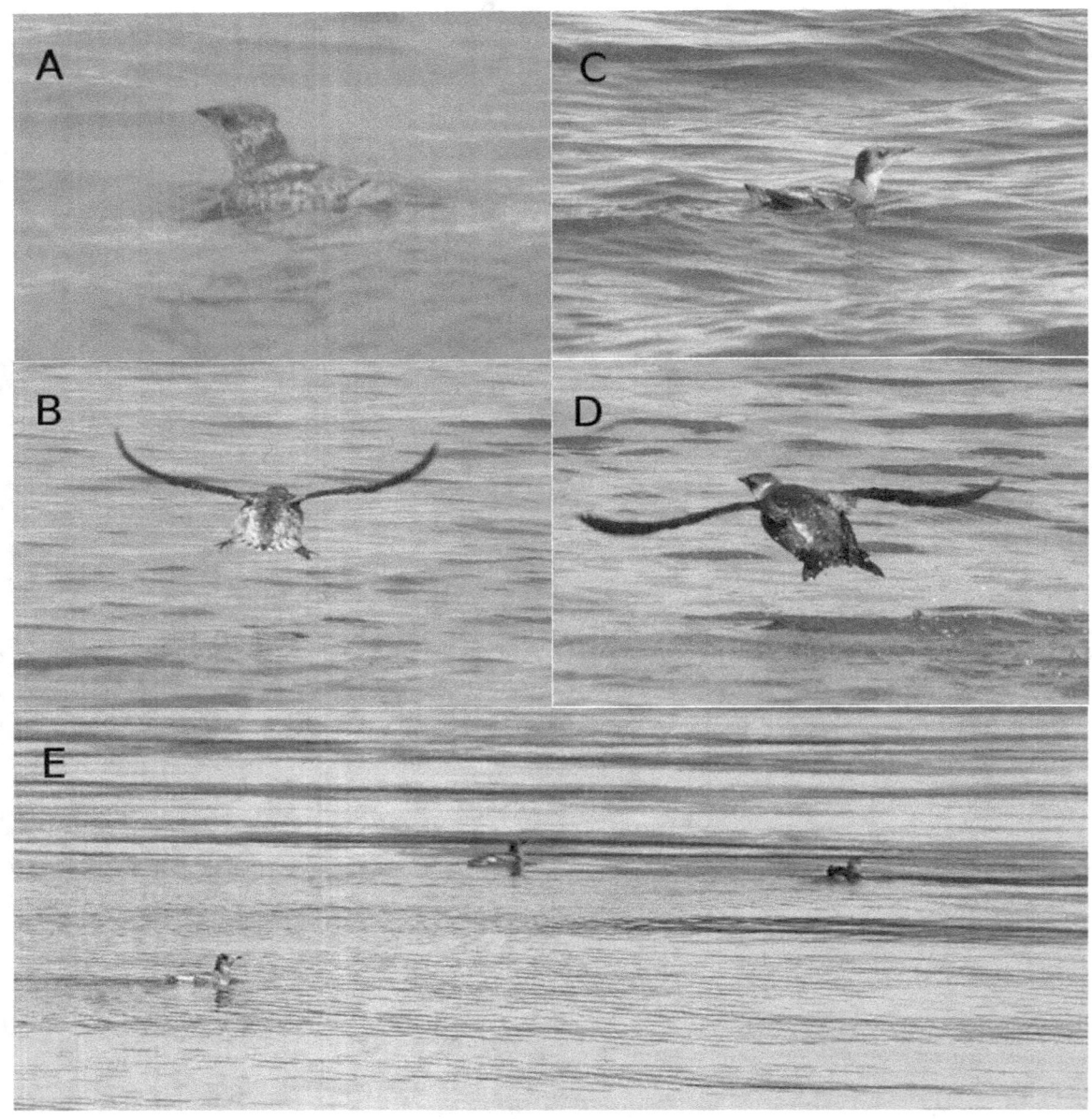

Figure 3. Kittlitz's murrelets (A, B) are about 30 cm in length and in breeding plumage are speckled in gray and white above; sandy, golden, or buff colors are also observed. Kittlitz's murrelets are distinguished from marbled murrelets by a shorter bill, lighter overall coloration (A), and white tips on central retrices and mostly white outer retrices, visible shortly after takeoff (B). Marbled murrelets have a longer bill and are typically russet to dark brown above (C) with dark retrices, but may have white upper tail coverts (D). The two may exist in mixed groups (E; 1 Kittlitz's murrelet on left) and cannot always reliably be distinguished in the field. Photos: B. J. Moynahan.

observer(s), who worked together to collect survey data. To estimate detection of groups near the center line, we added an independent observer, who did not interact with the primary observer(s).

The independent observer located groups of murrelets near the center line far ahead of the boat and recorded whether these focal groups were detected by primary observer(s) during the survey.

Analytic methods

We estimated probability of detection and species-specific abundance using Program DISTANCE version 6.0 (Thomas et al. 2010) following methods outlined by Buckland (2001). Because these methods assumed complete detection near the center line and could only be applied to murrelets identified to species, we also modified these methods as described by Hoekman et al. (2011b) to estimate species-specific density accounting for incomplete detection and identification. These adjustments assumed the proportion of each species in the identified and unidentified samples was the same and that species were correctly identified. To estimate abundance, we multiplied estimated densities by the area of our study (1,092 km^2). To facilitate comparison with previous strip transect surveys in Glacier Bay (that typically used 300 m strip widths, or 150 m on either side of the boat), we generated strip transect estimates by using only identified groups within 150 m of the center line and the separate ratio estimator of Cochran (1977). To assess number of observers relative to performance, we compared encounter rates and detection functions for transects that were randomly assigned 1 vs. 2 observers. We used logistic regression to estimate probability of detection near the center line as the proportion of focal groups detected by the independent observer that were also detected by the primary observer(s). To display the distribution of each species across surveyed transects, we plotted the location where each identified group was observed, with the diameter of each symbol proportional to group size.

Results

We surveyed 53 transects totaling 219.0 km between 8-15 July, 2009 and detected 1,064 groups (mean group size = 2.63, range = 1 to 61). We classified 151 (14%) and 348 (33%) groups as Kittlitz's and marbled murrelets and 565 (53%) groups as unidentified. Conditions were generally clear and calm during surveys, but observers had difficulty detecting and identifying murrelets when Beaufort sea state was 3. An extremely high number of Kittlitz's murrelets was encountered on 1 transect in the low density stratum surveyed by 2 observers; this outlier was removed from comparisons of 1 vs. 2 observers, but was included in abundance estimates. Encounter rates were 56% higher with 2 ($\bar{x} \pm$ SD; 3.74 $\pm$ 0.49 groups/km) relative to 1 (2.40 $\pm$ 0.57) observer (Fig. 4). For 1 observer, frequency of detections

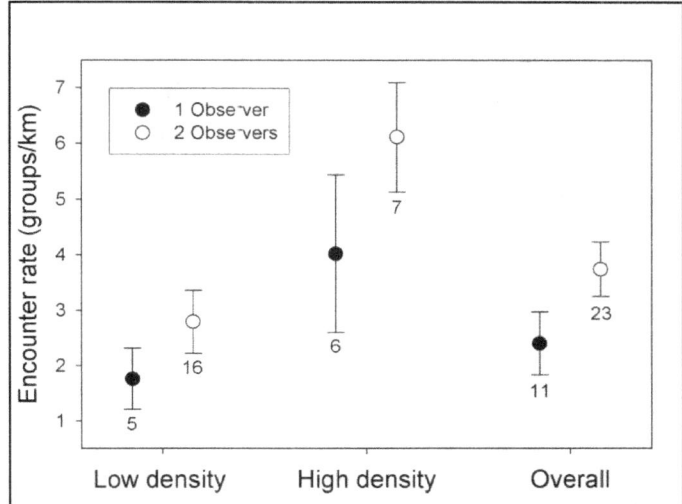

Figure 4. Estimated encounter rates (groups/km) from line transect surveys for combined Kittlitz's and marbled murrelets in low and high density strata with one versus two observers in Glacier Bay, July 2009. Samples of transects shown beneath estimates.

declined precipitously beyond 70 m from the center line (Fig. 5), and we were unable to generate a detection function with suitable goodness-of-fit as a result. In addition, species identification rates for 2 observers exceeded those for 1 by >20%.

We estimated probability of detection near the center line to be 0.94 $\pm$ 0.03. Our estimated detection function for all murrelets pooled showed probability of detection decayed rapidly with increasing distance from the center line, that detection was <50% at 150 m, and that the proportion of unidentified murrelets increased with distance. We observed >100% increases in density estimates and slight increases in estimated precision by accounting for both probability of detection near the center line and probability of identification (Table 1).

Density of Kittlitz's murrelets was nearly twice as high in the high density relative to low density stratum, but densities of marbled murrelets were similar between strata. Extrapolated across our study area, estimated abundance was 13,124 $\pm$ 4,062 Kittlitz's and 28,978 $\pm$ 4077 marbled murrelets. Our results for Kittlitz's murrelets were strongly influenced by a single transect in the low density stratum with a very high encounter rate; removal of this transect decreased density and abundance estimates and CVs by ~30%. Variation in encounter rates among transects dominated overall variance of density estimates for both species (Table 2). Estimated abundances using strip transect methods were substantially lower for Kittlitz's (5,624 $\pm$ 59), marbled (11,711 $\pm$ 432), and total murrelets (34,821 $\pm$ 1,333).

The distribution of Kittlitz's murrelets was clumped, with 3 primary hotspots across our transects (Fig. 6). The densest concentration was immediately west of the Beardslee Islands, with lesser concentrations within the high density stratum in the upper fjords south and west of Russell Island and in upper Muir Inlet. Marble Murrelets were uniformly common across the main bay and Muir Inlet, but were relatively sparse elsewhere (Fig. 7).

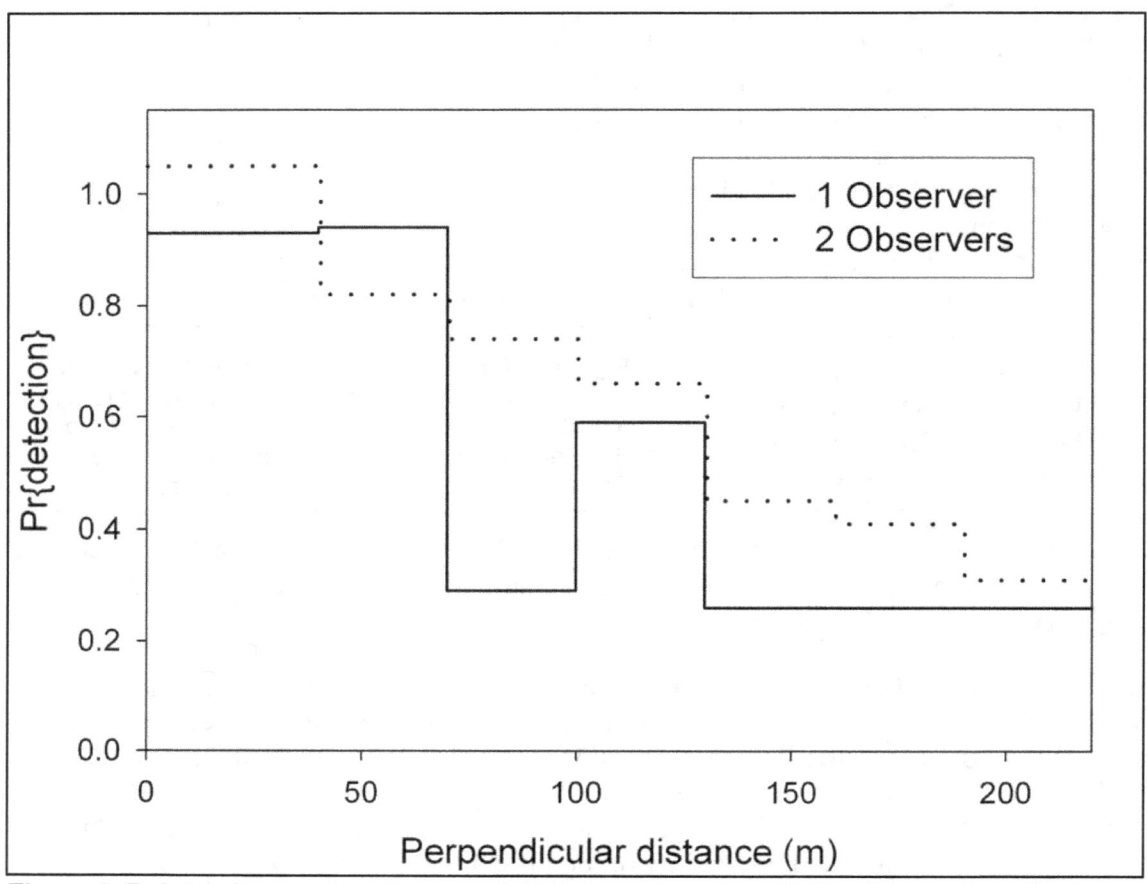

Figure 5. Relative frequencies of groups detected versus perpendicular distance from the transect center line with one (*n* = 131) versus two (*n* = 498) observers during line transect surveys for Kittlitz's and marbled murrelets in Glacier Bay, July 2009.

Table 1. Estimated densities (individuals/km^2) of murrelets identified to species and adjusted densities (accounting for unidentified groups) in Glacier Bay, July 2009. Coefficient of variation (CV) in parentheses. Change in adjusted relative to unadjusted estimates of density and CV are expressed as percentages.

Species	Density stratum[a]	Density	Adjusted Density	% change in density	% change in CV
Kittlitz's murrelet	Low	4.1 (0.55)	9.9 (0.47)	140	-14
	High	8.6 (0.31)	17.4 (0.29)	101	-5
	All	5.4 (0.34)	12.0 (0.31)	122	-9
Marbled murrelet	Low	11.5 (0.21)	26.8 (0.17)	133	-18
	High	12.2 (0.23)	26.0 (0.21)	114	-6
	All	11.7 (0.17)	26.5 (0.14)	127	-15

[a]Strata defined from expected densities of Kittlitz's murrelets.

Table 2. Percent contribution of each component parameter to the total estimated variance of density estimates of Kittlitz's and marbled murrelets in Glacier Bay, July 2009.

Species	Encounter rate[a]	Group size	Detection across transect[b]	Detection near transect[c]
Kittlitz's murrelet	92	7	<1	1
Marbled murrelet	85	6	4	5

[a]Groups encountered per km.
[b]Probability of detection within the right truncation distance, estimated from the detection function.
[c]Probability of detection near the center line, estimated from the independent observer experiment.

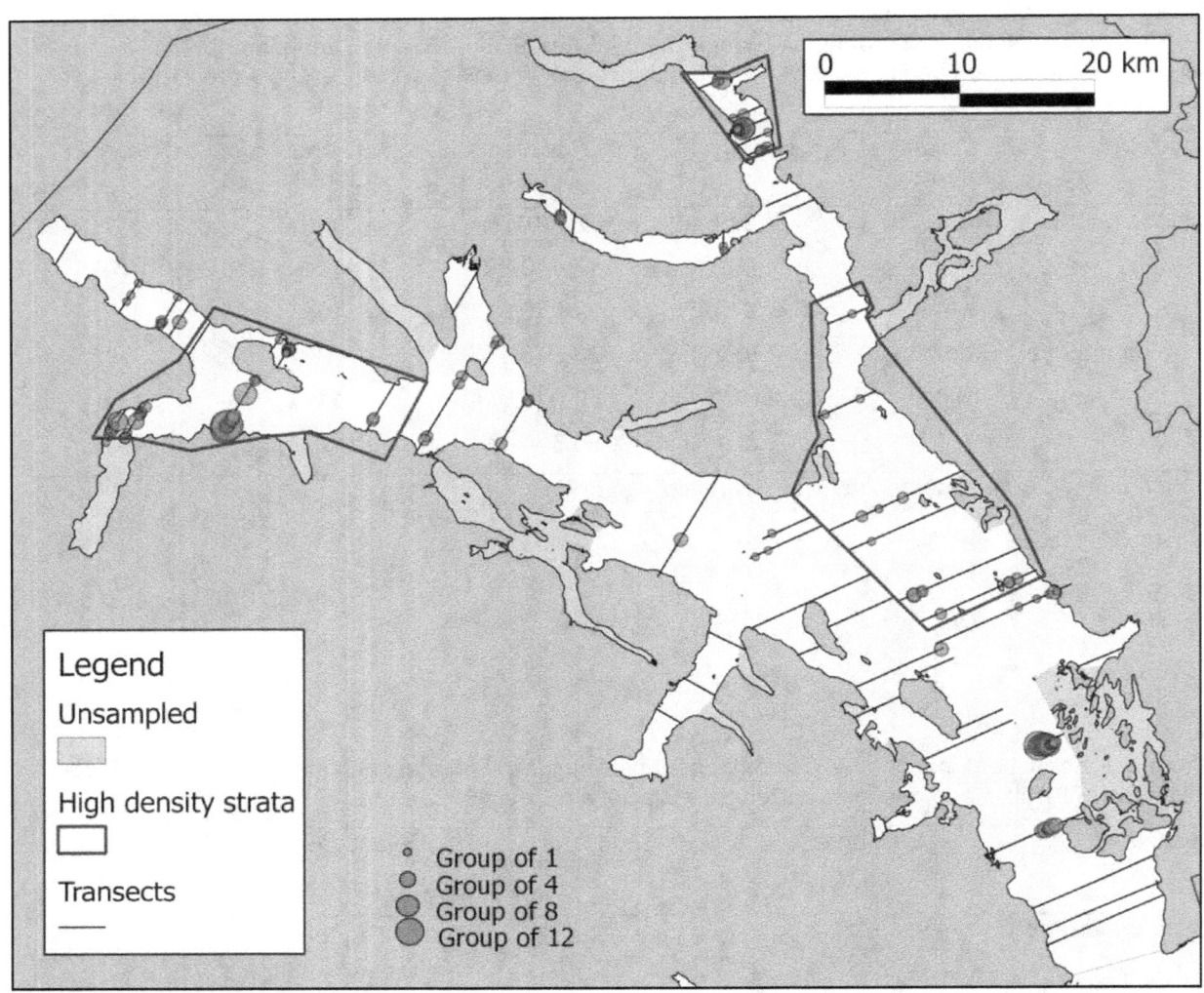

Figure 6. Distribution of observations of Kittlitz's murrelets along line transects in Glacier Bay, July 2009. The diameter of symbols is proportional to the size of the group. Blue lines circumscribe high density stratum. Areas shaded red were unsampled.

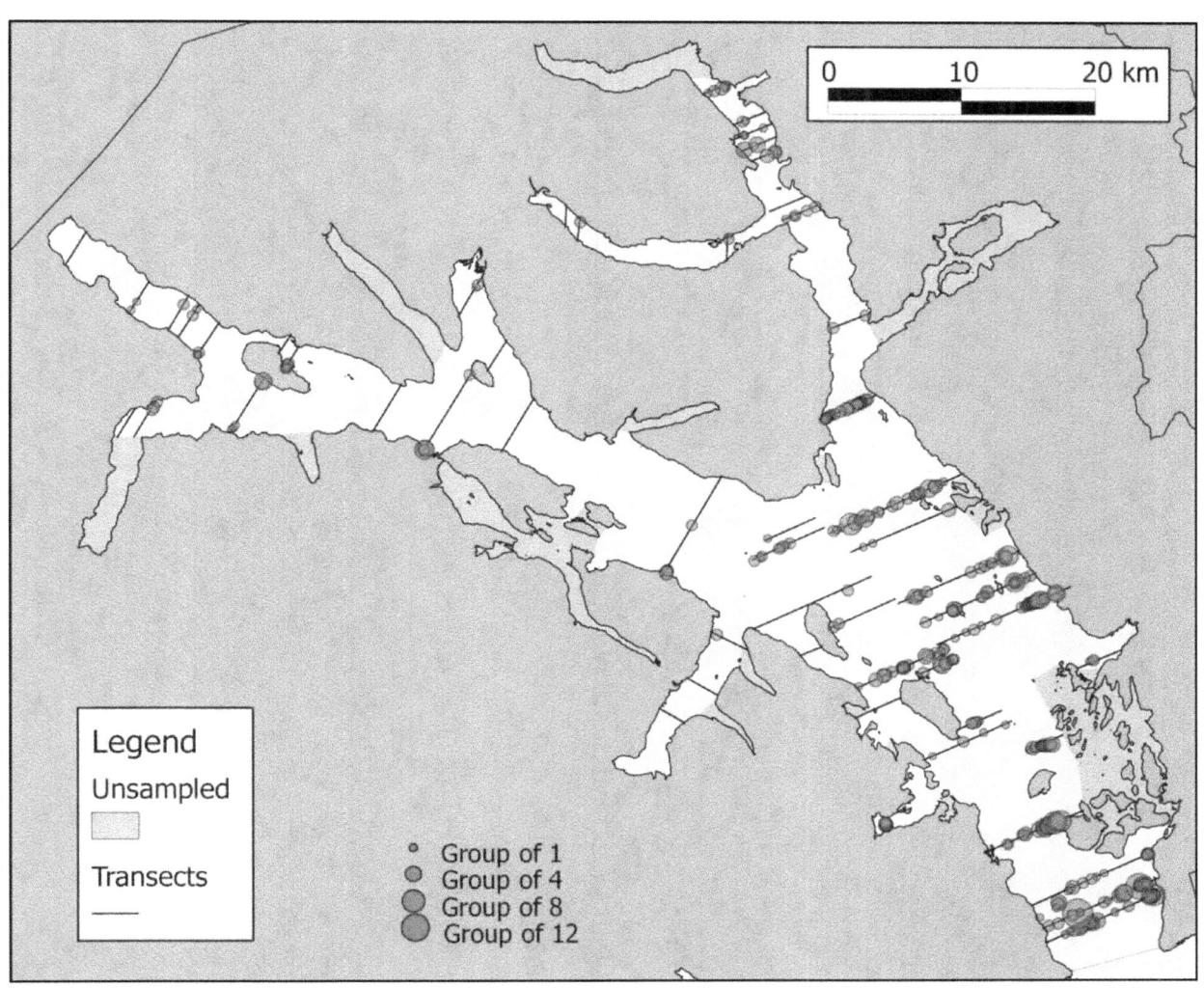

Figure 7. Distribution of observations of marbled murrelets along survey transects in Glacier Bay, July 2009. The diameter of symbols is proportional to the size of the group. Areas shaded red were unsampled.

Discussion

Line transect sampling allows estimation of probability of detection and hence is better suited to monitoring status and trends of murrelet populations in Glacier Bay than strip transect sampling. Strip transects for murrelets typically have employed 300 m strip widths (Gould and Forsell 1989, Drew et al. 2008). Observations of detection probability <1 and variation in detection relative to observer and climatic conditions within this distance (Mack et al. 2002, Kissling et al. 2007, Kirchhoff 2008, Ronconi and Burger 2009, Hoekman et al. 2011a, this study) indicated abundance estimates from strip transects likely suffer from large and variable negative bias. However, our estimates of abundance from line transect surveys would also be subject to negative bias if we did not account for detection <1 near the center line and incomplete species identification. Furthermore, we stress that all estimates of abundance in marine environments fail to include adults on nests, which comprise an unknown proportion of the population that likely varies relative to breeding propensity and nest success.

Abundance estimates for murrelets in this and other studies typically have been relatively imprecise, primarily on account of large variation in encounter rates among transects. This variation has been driven by highly aggregated distributions observed for Kittlitz's murrelets in this and other studies in Glacier Bay (Drew et al. 2008, Kirchhoff et al. 2010). Our estimated densities in the high density stratum were almost twice that in low density stratum, indicating that stratification improved precision. However, a high outlier in the low density stratum accounted for almost a third of the total variance in estimated abundance and substantially decreased effectiveness of stratification. The transect length for this outlier (2.6 km) was below the average (4.1), and maintaining more uniform transect lengths likely would mitigate variation in encounter rates associated with local aggregations. The somewhat unpredictable annual variation in distribution of this species in Glacier Bay may limit utility of geographic strata. Similar distributions observed during concurrent strip transects conducted by Kirchhoff et al. (2010) suggested patterns persisted over the survey period. Distributions were dissimilar between species, and hence our strategy of optimal allocation of sampling effort for Kittlitz's murrelets will be suboptimal for marbled murrelets.

Our estimate of ~15,000 Kittlitz's murrelets on the water in Glacier Bay represents a substantial fraction of the current, though recognized as inexact, global population estimate of 31,000-57,000 birds (USFWS 2010). Our abundance estimates exceeded other recent estimates from Glacier Bay (which have ranged from 2,500-5,300 birds) by three- to six-fold. However, differences in survey timing, sampling area, and survey methods complicated comparisons between our and others' results. In particular, previous studies – in Glacier Bay and elsewhere – commonly used strip transect methods that under-estimate abundance, and it remains uncertain whether our relatively high recent abundance estimates for Glacier Bay reflected population increases, sampling error, or differences in methods. We urge care in interpretation of our density and abundance estimates on account of their precision, the pilot nature of the 2009 survey, and differences in methods relative to previous studies. See Hoekman et al. (2011a) for a more in depth comparison. It is clear, however, that Glacier Bay is clearly of substantial importance to this species, globally and regionally.

Low precision of estimates for Kittlitz's murrelets weakened inference about population status and trend, and three factors contributed to identification rates that were less than desired during these pilot surveys: observer inexperience in 2009, large sighting distances, and our protocol of classifying groups as identified only when confidence was high. If the assumption that the proportion of each species in the identified and unidentified samples was the same was reasonable, bias in abundance estimates resulting from low identification rates likely was low. However, even modest levels of mis-identification could introduce substantial bias (Hoekman et al. 2011b, Kirchhoff *In Review*). A benefit of statistically accounting for unidentified murrelets is that, when uncertainty in identification exists, observers may better balance the relatively low risk from classifying birds as unidentified versus the potentially higher risk from mis-identifying birds. Achieving high and accurate identification rates through training and evaluation of observers is paramount to maximizing reliability of results.

Similar to Mack et al. (2002), we found detection of murrelets near the center line was slightly <1. Murrelets near the center line may go undetected because they fly or swim away while the approaching boat is still at a large distance (100+ m) or because they pass beneath the boat during a prolonged (20+ s) dive. Lukacs et al (2010) found a survey speed of 10 km/h limited the probability of failing to detect diving birds, and our high detection rate at this speed was consistent with their conclusion. However, distance sampling relies on the critical assumption of complete detection near the center line to estimate abundance and to justify the assumption of pooling robustness in estimation of detection functions (Buckland et al. 2001). Detection <1 will result in biased estimates of abundance, but accounting for probability of detection near the center line when estimating abundance will minimize bias. We recommend periodically calibrating estimated probability of detection relative to likely sources of variation, such as different observers and environmental conditions (Mack et al. 2002, Ronconi and Burger 2009).

Strip and line transect surveys for murrelets and other marine birds have typically utilized either 1 (Gould and Forsell 1989, Ralph and Miller 1995) or 2 (Raphael et al. 2007, Drew et al. 2008) observers. Differences in performance have rarely been assessed, but Mack et al. (2002) found some evidence of higher detection probability with 2 observers during murrelet surveys. The large reduction in encounters we observed for 1 relative to 2 observers will slightly reduce precision of abundance estimates. More importantly, the sharp decrease in frequencies of detections at intermediate distances for surveys using 1 observer resulted in data that violated shape criteria required for robust estimation of detection probability (Buckland et al. 2001). Increased rates of species identification with 2 observers likely resulted from decreased task saturation and lessened the magnitude of the assumption used to account for unidentified murrelets.

Continuously counting flying murrelets would produce biased estimates because flying birds violate two assumptions of line transect sampling: they move rapidly relative to the speed of the observer, and they evade observers (Buckland et al. 2001). Other problems with continuous counts over unlimited distances were that flying groups could be located at very large distances (up to 1 km), could rarely be identified to species, and distracted observers from locating nearby groups on the water. We tested various potential methods for obtaining unbiased estimates of densities of flying birds on an *ad hoc* basis. One option was to count birds that pass through a moving 2-dimensional plane extending at right angles from the path of the boat. However, many birds crossing perpendicular to the path of the boat appeared to alter their path to pass ~100 m ahead of or behind the boat, thus biasing this method. Another alternative is to conduct snapshot counts, which are instantaneous counts over a specified area. This method could produce good results if the area was large enough to encompass evasive movements of flying birds. However, given past encounter rates for flying birds, we estimated that suitable precision would require snapshot counts every ~60 s, which we felt would require a dedicated observer to avoid degrading performance in counting birds on the water. In lieu of adding another observer, we recommend continuously counting flying groups within a fixed distance (200 m) that encompasses evasive movements of flying birds. While not useful for estimating density, this index to the population of flying birds would allow estimation of trend over time and would not place undue burden on observers.

Recommendations

Below are specific recommendations for 2010 surveys for Kittlitz's murrelets in Glacier Bay:

- Line transect sampling is an appropriate survey method and should be preferred to strip transect sampling.

- Develop a pool of observers skilled in murrelet detection and identification.

- Account for incomplete species identification in species-specific abundance estimates.

- Prefer the use of 2 (or more) observers relative to 1.

- Survey design should incorporate spatially-balanced sampling.

- Increase sampling effort where expected densities of Kittlitz's murrelets are high.

- Use analytic methods that do not rely on *a priori* delineation of strata.

- Reduce maximum Beaufort sea state for surveys from 3 to 2.

- Periodically calibrate estimates of probability near the center line for different observers and environmental conditions.

- Train observers regularly in distance estimation using laser range finders.

- Strive to keep transect lengths in the 4-8 km range.

Literature Cited

Agler, B. A., S. J. Kendall, and D. B. Irons. 1998. Abundance and distribution of marbled and Kittlitz's murrelets in south central and southeast Alaska. Condor 100:254-265.

Agness, A. M., J. F. Piatt, J. C. Ha, and G. R. VanBlaricom. 2008. Effects of vessel activity on the near-shore ecology of Kittlitz's Murrelets (*Brachyramphus brevirostris*) in Glacier Bay, Alaska. Auk 125:346-353.

Bachler, E., and F. Liechti. 2007. On the importance of g(0) for estimating bird population densities with standard distance-sampling: Implications from a telemetry study and a literature review. Ibis 149:693-700.

Buckland, S. T., D. R. Anderson, K. P. Burnham, J. L. Laake, D. L. Borchers, and L. Thomas. 2001. Introduction to Distance Sampling: Estimating Abundance of Biological Populations. Oxford University Press, New York, New York, USA.

Cochran, W. G. 1977. Sampling Techniques, 3rd edition. Wiley, New York, New York.

Day, R. H. 1995. New information on Kittlitz's Murrelet Nests. Condor 97:271-273.

Day, R. H., K. J. Kuletz, and D. A. Nigro. 1999. Kittlitz's murrelet (Brachyramphus brevirostris), The Birds of North America Online (A. Poole, Ed.). Ithaca: Cornell Lab of Ornithology; Available at Birds of North America Online: http://bna.birds.cornell.edu/bna/species/435.

Drew, G. S., S. Speckman,, J. F. Piatt, J. M. Burgos, and J. Bodkin. 2008. Survey Design Considerations for Monitoring Marine Predator Populations in Glacier Bay, Alaska: Results and Post-hoc Analyses of Surveys Conducted in 1999-2003. Administrative Report. U. S. Department of the Interior, U. S. Geological Survey, Reston, Virginia.

Fewster, R., S. Buckland, K. Burnham, D. Borchers, P. Jupp, J. Laake, and L. Thomas. 2009. Estimating the encounter rate variance in distance sampling. Biometrics 65:225-236.

Gould, P. J., and D. J. Forsell. 1989. Techniques for shipboard surveys of marine birds. Fish and Wildlife Technical Report 25. U. S. Department of the Interior, U. S. Fish and Wildlife Service, Washington, D.C.

Hoekman, S. T., B. J. Moynahan, and M. S. Lindberg. 2011a. Monitoring Kittlitz's and marbled murrelets in Glacier Bay National Park: 2010 Annual Report. Southeast Alaska Network, National Park Service, Juneau, AK.

Hoekman, S., B. J. Moynahan, M. S. Lindberg, L. C. Sharman, and W. F. Johnson. 2011b. Line transect sampling for Murrelets: Accounting for incomplete detection and identification. Marine Ornithology 39:xxx-xxx.

Kirchhoff, M. D. *In Review*. On improving the power and accuracy of surveys for Kittlitz's murrelets *Brachyramphus brevirostris* in Alaska. Marine Ornithology 39:xx-xx.

Kirchhoff, M. 2008. Methodological considerations for at-sea monitoring of *Brachyramphus* murrelets in Glacier Bay, Alaska. Alaska Department of Fish and Game, Unpublished Report, Douglas, Alaska.

Kirchhoff, M. D., M. Smith, and S. Wright. 2010. Abundance, population trend, and distribution of Marbled Murrelets and Kittlitz's Murrelets in Glacier Bay National Park. Audubon Alaska, Unpublished report, Anchorage, Alaska.

Kissling, M. L., M. Reid, P. M. Lukacs, S. M. Gende, and S. B. Lewis. 2007. Understanding abundance patterns of a declining seabird: Implications for monitoring. Ecological Applications 17:2164-2174.

Kuletz, K. J., S. W. Stephensen, D. B. Irons, E. A. Labunski, and K. M. Brenneman. 2003. Changes in distribution and abundance of Kittlitz's murrelets *Brachyramphus breviostris* relative to glacial recession in Prince William Sound, Alaska. Marine Ornithology 31:133-140.

Lindell, J. R. 2005. Results of at-sea *Brachyramphus* murrelet surveys in Icy Strait and other selected areas of southeast Alaska, 1993-1999. U.S. Fish and Wildlife Service, Juneau, Alaska.

Lukacs, P. M., M. L. Kissling, M. Reid, S. M. Gende, and S. B. Lewis. 2010. Testing assumptions of distance sampling on a pelagic seabird. Condor 112:455-459.

Mack, D. E., M. G. Raphael, and J. L. Laake. 2002. Probability of detecting marbled murrelets at sea: Effects of single versus paired observers. Journal of Wildlife Management 66:865-873.

Moynahan, B. J., W. F. Johnson, D. W. Shirokauer, L. C. Sharman, G. Smith, and S. M. Gende. 2008. Vital Sign Monitoring Plan: Southeast Alaska Network. U. S. National Park Service, Fort Collins, Colorado.

Ralph, C. J., and S. L. Miller. 1995. Offshore population estimates of marbled murrelets in California. Pages 353-360 *in* Ecology and conservation of the Marbled Murrelet. General Technical Report PSW-GTR-152. U.S. Department of Agriculture, U. S. Forest Service, Pacific Southwest Research Station, Albany, California.

Raphael, M. G., J. Baldwin, G. A. Falxa, M. H. Huff, M. Lance, S. L. Miller, S. F. Pearson, C. J. Ralph, C. Strong, and C. Thompson. 2007. Regional population monitoring of the Marbled Murrelet: Field and analytical methods. U.S. Department of Agriculture, U. S. Forest Service, Pacific Northwest Research Station, Portland, Oregon.

Robards, M., G. Drew, J. Piatt, M. Anson, A. Abookire, J. Bodkin, P. Hooge, and S. Speckman. 2003. Ecology of selected marine communities in Glacier bay: Zooplankton, forage fish, seabirds and marine mammals. U. S. Geological Survey, Alaska Science Center, Biological Sciences Office, Anchorage, Alaska.

Romano, M. D., J. F. Piatt, G. S. Drew, and J. L. Bodkin. 2007. Temporal and Spatial Variability in Distribution of Kittlitz's Murrelet in Glacier Bay. Pages 117-119 *in* Proceedings of the

Fourth Glacier Bay Science Symposium. U.S. Geological Survey, Reston, Virginia, Juneau, Alaska.

Ronconi, R. A., and A. E. Burger. 2009. Estimating seabird densities from vessel transects: Distance sampling and implications for strip transects. Aquatic Biology 4:297-309.

Thomas, L., S. T. Buckland, E. A. Rexstad, J. L. Laake, S. Strincberg, S. L. Hedley, J. R. Bishop, T. A. Marques, and K. P. Burnham. 2010. Distance software: Design and analysis of distance sampling surveys for estimating population size. Journal of Applied Ecology 47:5-14.

U. S. Fish and Wildlife Service (USFWS). 2010. Species assessment and listing priority assignment form for Kittlitz's murrelets. Unpublished document. U. S. Fish and Wildlife Service, Anchorage, Alaska.

Williams, B. K., J. D. Nichols, and M. J. Conroy. 2002. Analysis and Management of Animal Populations, 1st edition. Academic Press, San Diego, California.

National Park Service
U.S. Department of the Interior

Natural Resource Program Center
1201 Oakridge Drive, Suite 150
Fort Collins, CO 80525

www.nature.nps.gov

EXPERIENCE YOUR AMERICA ™